1 When did language begin?

Animal communication

Did you know that our human **ancestors** were similar to apes? Apes are a group of animals that includes gorillas and chimpanzees. Just as apes can't talk, our ancestors couldn't either. Apes make different sounds, but they mostly communicate with one another using hand gestures and facial expressions.

Have you been able to communicate with someone who doesn't speak your language by using gestures, such as pointing and smiling? Perhaps you have had to communicate with a friend in a loud place, like a school disco. We can communicate a lot of things without words!

Humans start to speak

Fossils of early humans show that their throats weren't able to make the sounds that modern humans can. Speech became possible when modern humans **evolved**, somewhere between 50,000 and 100,000 years ago.

As early humans developed, they began to have more and more reasons to need language. For example, early humans began to develop tools to help them with work, such as hunting, cooking and building.

Human evolution

If your hands are busy using tools, you can't use them to make gestures to tell other people what you're thinking or what you want them to do. If you need to communicate when it's too dark to see, or when your friends are far away, gestures alone aren't much help. That's when speech came in! We don't know what the first words were, but the language would have been a very simple one.

Language is power!

Most animals have adapted to live in a particular habitat, but humans can live in almost every environment in the world, from hot deserts to the icy Arctic. To be able to do that, we have to share our knowledge and skills – and for that, we need language.

Everything around you needs specialised knowledge and skills to make – from the toothbrush you use in the morning to the bed you sleep in at night. Over time, humans have gradually invented and improved these items, and handed down the knowledge and skills to make them from one generation to the next. At first, people passed on their skills **verbally**, then later they were passed on in writing. It's language that has allowed humans to share and develop their skills over time.

Contents

Welcome 2
1. When did language begin? 3
2. How did writing begin? 10
3. Modern writing 16
4. Languages in danger! 19
5. Where is English from? 31
6. Anglophone countries 37
7. Indigenous British languages 43
8. Culture 48
9. Printing 56
10. Other kinds of languages 63
    Glossary 70
    Index 71

Welcome

Hello, I'm Kaya and I love language! My grandparents come from the UK, Madagascar, Nepal and New Zealand, so I hear a lot of different languages in my family!

Have you ever wondered why there are so many languages? Did you know that languages change over time, and that some even die? Or that some languages spoken on opposite sides of the world use similar words?

Have you ever heard people speaking the same language but sounding different, and wondered where **accents** come from?

Have you ever thought about who was the first to have the idea to write words down?

Have you ever looked at a word and wondered where it came from?

Let's find out about all of this together! We need to start by going back in time 150,000 years ...

World languages

There are about 7,000 languages spoken around the world, but about half the people in the world speak just ten languages between them.

💡 Did you know?

These are the ten most spoken languages in the world.

- Mandarin
- Spanish
- English
- Arabic
- Hindi
- Bengali
- Portuguese
- Russian
- Japanese
- Lahnda (Western Punjabi)

Languages spoken around the world can sound very different from each other, but there are some things they have in common.

- **QUESTIONS:** Have you ever noticed that when someone is asking a question, their voice usually goes up at the end? Even if you can't understand the language someone is speaking, you can often tell when they ask a question because most languages do this.

Do you know anyone who speaks the same language as you but with a different accent?

- **ACCENT:** Everyone speaks with an accent, which usually depends on the area where you lived when you started to speak. All languages can be spoken with different accents.

- **HUH:** Most languages have one word in common, which sounds like a question. Wherever you are in the world, if you say 'Huh?' the person you are talking to will know that you haven't understood something they've said.

> ### 💡 Did you know?
> Another word that is similar in many languages is the word for *tea*. Tea was first **exported** from China, where it was called *te* – so you can see where the English word comes from!

💡 Did you know?
Every sentence we speak, in any language, contains a subject, a verb and an object. For example:

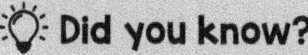

In English, we normally put words in this order: subject–verb–object, but most languages use a different word order: subject–object–verb. This would sound like:

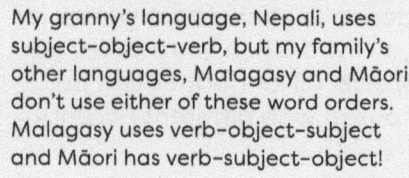

> My granny's language, Nepali, uses subject–object–verb, but my family's other languages, Malagasy and Māori, don't use either of these word orders. Malagasy uses verb–object–subject and Māori has verb–subject–object!

- **REGISTER:** All languages have ways of being expressed more politely or more informally, depending on who you're talking to and whether you're speaking or writing. Think about how you speak to your teachers and to your friends.

- **CHANGE:** Languages change over time. Maybe your parents or grandparents use words that you don't use because they sound old-fashioned to you, and you may use words that people older than you don't say.

- **GRAMMAR:** Grammar is about different word types, such as nouns, verbs, adjectives and adverbs, and how these word types are combined to make a sentence. Grammar is important because it allows us to talk about the past, the present and the future. It provides rules and structures for expressing our feelings and ideas.

Language families

We can divide the world's 7,000 languages into 147 families or groups of languages. Each family or group has a single language they all come from – a bit like how brothers and sisters may share the same parents – but language family trees go back thousands of years.

Do some family members look a bit like you? They may have the same hair or eye colour, but not look exactly like you. It's the same in language families – some languages in a family have similar words.

If you trace language family trees back far enough, eventually you'll come to the first language that all languages came from.

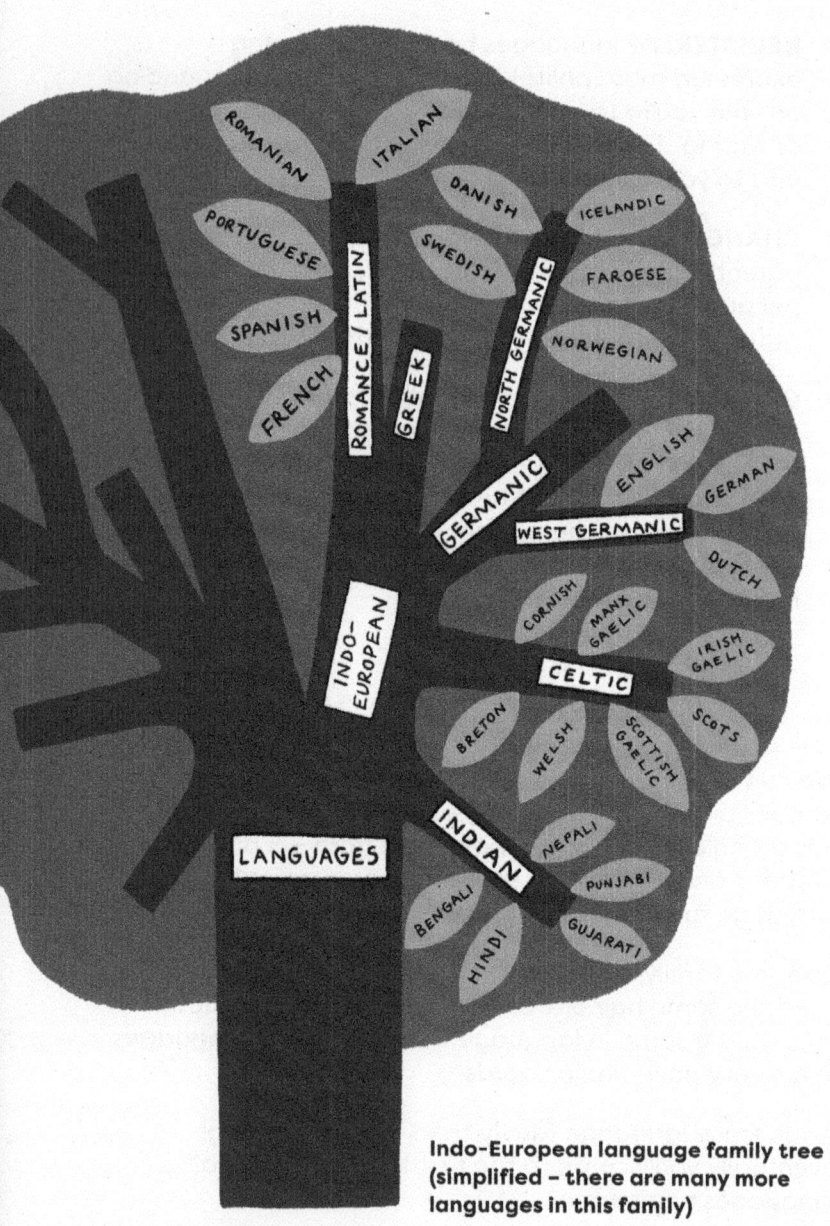

Indo-European language family tree (simplified – there are many more languages in this family)

As the people who spoke the first language moved around the world, their language developed and changed, as all languages do. Very gradually, over many thousands of years, new languages formed in different parts of the world from this first language. Every language continued to develop and form new languages as people moved to different places. Languages continue to change to this day!

Have you ever drawn your family tree to show how your family members are related? We can also draw a tree of languages to show how different language groups are related to each other. Have a look at the simplified tree opposite.

It would need a big tree to show 147 families and 7,000 languages, so we're focusing on one family of languages – the Indo-European language family. These are languages that are **native** to much of Europe and South Asia, and are also spoken in parts of America, Africa and Oceania.

The Indo-European language family has the most speakers spread over the largest area on Earth of any of the language families. There are about 450 languages in this family, spoken by 3 billion people, which is nearly half of the world!

Indo-European languages come from an older language called Proto-Indo-European, which was spoken around 8,000 years ago in Turkey. Very gradually, over thousands of years, the Proto-Indo-European language evolved and formed new languages as the people who spoke it moved from Turkey to other parts of Europe and South Asia.

> Proto-Indo-European was never written down. When did people first start to write? Let's find out!

❷ How did writing begin?

We've talked about the beginnings of languages, but when did people first start to write them down?

People have been writing for at least 5,000 years! That's since around 3000 BCE.

Unlike animals, people can talk about the past and future and about different places. Writing takes us a step further – we can write down our thoughts for someone else to read. That person may then read them in a different place and at a different time. We can even read texts that were written hundreds or thousands of years ago, and the things we write today could be read years into the future.

 Did you know?

History is anything that's in the past, but *prehistory* is history before anything was written down.

The first writing

The earliest writing – although it doesn't look much like today's writing – appeared in Mesopotamia around 3000 BCE.

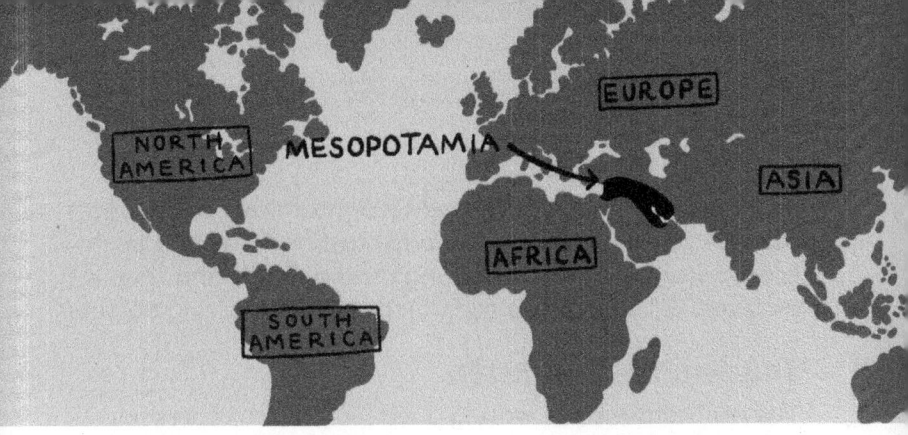

Until around 3000 BCE, most people in Mesopotamia had to grow their own food to survive. However, improved farming techniques meant that they no longer needed to do this, and people started to barter to exchange goods. Barter is where people swap extra goods they've produced for other goods they want or need. Money hadn't been invented yet, so people were paid for their work in goods. So, a farmer might pay his farm workers by giving them some of his crops. **Taxes** were paid the same way.

This clay tablet shows cuneiform writing that says how much barley farm labourers were given as payment for their work.

Rulers needed to keep a record of the goods people produced so that they knew what everyone had to pay. Records were written on clay tablets using a very simple form of writing called *cuneiform*. Cuneiform consisted of a simple picture of produce, such as a crop or animal, next to circles that represented numbers.

Barley is a crop farmers grow. It is used to make food such as bread.

Ancient Egypt

Around the same time as the Mesopotamians, 5,700 years ago, Ancient Egyptians were also starting to write. Like in Mesopotamia, Egyptian writing used symbols and simple pictures, which were painted on pottery and stone objects.

The Narmer Palette

The earliest forms of writing used pictures to represent objects, like the barley in the clay tablet on page 11. People did not yet write about more abstract things, such as time and emotions. The first big advance in writing came when people used pictures not to mean the object being shown, but to stand for another word that sounded the same. This type of writing was found in a tomb in Egypt on a carved stone tray called the *Narmer Palette*.

Narmer was the first **pharaoh** of Egypt. How do we know his name? The tray found in his tomb includes small icons, called *pictograms*. Next to a picture of a king are small pictograms of a catfish and a chisel. The Egyptian for 'catfish' is *nar* and 'chisel' is *mer*. This tells us the king's name: *Narmer*! This is the first known period in time when people used symbols to represent sounds, rather than drawing pictures of the thing they were writing about.

Catfish and chisels have nothing to do with the pharaoh except that they give the sounds of his name!

Egyptian hieroglyphs and hieroglyphics

Out of the pictograms came the world's first true writing system. Egyptian **hieroglyphics** use simple pictures (**hieroglyphs**) not only to mean the item in the picture, but also to represent the sound of that word, as in *Narmer*.

The earliest complete Egyptian text was found in the tomb of a pharaoh called Teti, who died around 2300 BCE. The image below shows part of the hieroglyphics found in his tomb. What objects and animals can you see?

This spells Teti. We know that it's a royal name because the Ancient Egyptians wrote royal names inside ovals.

Early writing systems around the world

The Mesopotamians and Egyptians were writing in this way 5,000 years ago, but they weren't the only people to capture language in writing.

Over 3,000 years ago, the Shang emperors in China were using simple pictures to record their language in a way that is very similar to modern Chinese writing.

A few centuries later, around 600 BCE, the Maya people in Central America also developed a picture-based writing system.

How did people from around the world all have similar picture-based writing systems when they were so far away from each other and are unlikely to have met? This was not an idea that spread from one place. Instead, people across the world came up with similar ideas about how to write down their languages.

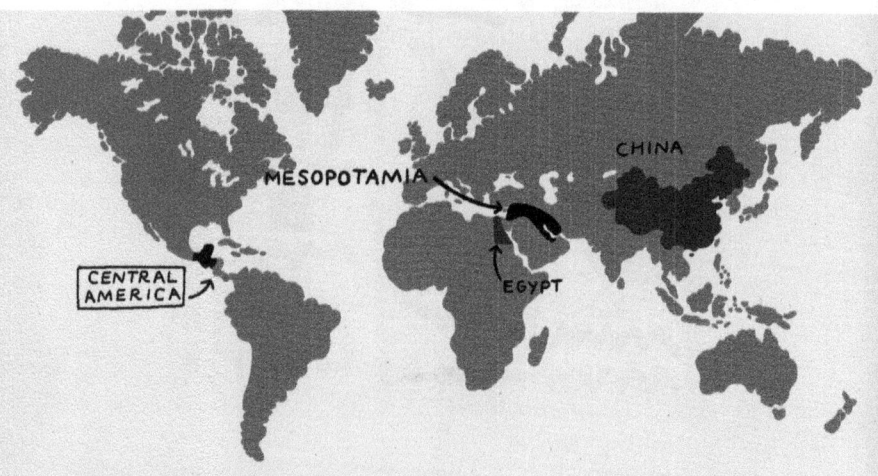

These places developed picture-based writing systems between around 3700 BCE and 600 BCE.

The first alphabet

The first alphabet was discovered in the Sinai desert in Egypt. Alphabets are made up of letters rather than pictograms. This alphabet was used, not by local Egyptians, but by people from Canaan (a region to the northeast of Egypt), who came to Egypt to trade goods. But how did they turn pictograms into letters?

They saw the Egyptian hieroglyphs and adapted them to their own language, then took them a step further. Instead of using a picture to represent the sound of the word, they used it to mean only the first sound of the word.

For example, they took the Egyptian hieroglyph of a bull. 'Bull' in the Canaanite language was *aleph*. They used this symbol to mean only the first sound of that word: /a/.	⌅
They did this for all the sounds in their language. For example, 'head' was *rosh*. So they used the Egyptian hieroglyph of a head. It came to mean /r/ in the Canaanite language.	ᕤ
Let's look at one more. What do you think this hieroglyph represents? It's water, which was *mem*. And so, it came to represent the sound /m/.	∿∿

Suddenly, only 25 to 30 pictures were needed to represent all the sounds in the Canaanite language.

> How did we get all the different alphabets people use around the world today?

3 Modern writing

Canaanite workers in Egypt took their new idea of writing back to Canaan. From there, travelling **traders** spread the system across the Middle East and Mediterranean, where it was picked up by the Ancient Greeks and Romans. As it spread, the letters were adapted for each language and simplified. Let's have a look at how.

Letter formation

Do you remember the bull used in Canaanite writing for the /a/ sound?	४
It was simplified and rotated.	⚹
And rotated again to become our letter A!	A

What about the head that Canaanite writing used for the /r/ sound?	ᖴ
This was simplified.	◁
You can see the beginnings of the letter R if you flip it over.	R

| And can you see how water, which represented the /m/ sound in Canaanite writing, became M? | |

Many languages developed their own letters from the Canaanite system. These alphabets made writing much easier, so more people were able to learn to read and write.

Latin alphabet

One of the alphabets that developed from the Canaanite system of writing is called the Latin alphabet. It's used for English and lots of other languages, like Italian and Icelandic.

The alphabet we use for English has 26 letters. Italian uses only 21 of them (it doesn't use j, k, w, x or y). And Icelandic has 32 letters!

Two of the letters that Icelandic uses are to distinguish between the different ways we say /th/.

💡 Did you know?

The Icelandic letter þ (called *thorn*) is said like the *th* at the start of the word *thorn*.

The letter ð (called *eth*) is said like the *th* in *these*.

Greek has two different letters for *th* too: ϑ (*theta*, said like in *thorn*) and ∂ (*delta*, said like in *these*).

Other alphabets

We'll meet some other languages throughout the book. Let's look at how one of them is written down.

Other alphabets have origins in the Canaanite system, but they developed very differently from the Latin alphabet. One of these is the Devanagari script that is used to write down languages in India and Nepal.

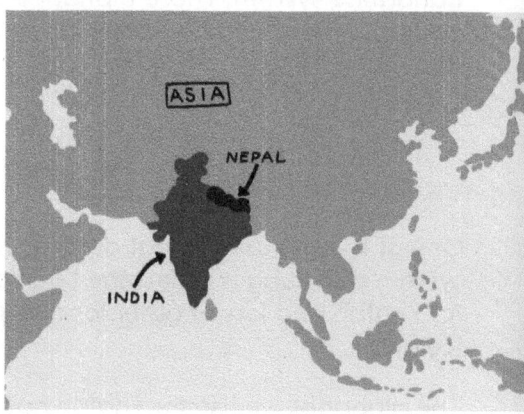

We've already looked at some hieroglyphs and how they changed to become letters we use today. For the Devanagari script, they developed rather differently.

Hieroglyph	Canaanite	Devanagari	Latin
𓂉	𐤀	अ	A
〰	𐤌	म	M
𓁹	𐤓	र	R

Let's have a look at some ancient languages and some languages that disappeared before they were ever written down.

4 Languages in danger!

It's not just animals that can be in danger of extinction – languages can disappear too!

Why languages die

Languages such as English or Mandarin that are spoken by millions of people are unlikely to die out. But sometimes,

> ### 💡 Did you know?
> A language dies every two weeks somewhere in the world.

when relatively few people speak a language, that language can disappear. For example, sometimes the community that speaks a language gets smaller and smaller, until there are only one or two speakers of the language left. When the last speaker of a language dies, their language usually disappears too.

Another way in which languages are lost is when other people with a different language arrive in a place and take over.

From the 15th century, many European countries **colonised** other parts of the world. This is partly why languages that come from Europe, such as English, French, Spanish, Portuguese and Dutch, are spoken in countries all around the world.

Once a country was colonised, the language of the people who took over became the dominant language. Sometimes, local people were allowed to work only if they spoke the new language, and schools could be forced to teach all their classes using it.

When people no longer use their native language, they can start to forget it in only a few months.

The languages we speak are part of our identity. They are how we think and how we communicate with our family and friends. They also allow us to relate to other people who speak the same language.

> ## 💡 Did you know?
> Before colonisation, around 300 languages were spoken in Australia. Only around 200 are left, and just 12 of those are still being taught to children, so the other languages are at risk of dying out.
>
> It's a similar story on the American continents. Around 300 languages were spoken before colonisation, but about half have disappeared.

How might you feel if you couldn't use your own language any longer?

Dead languages

A *dead* language may still be used or studied, but no one speaks it as a native language. Three of the most famous dead languages are Latin, Ancient Greek and Sanskrit. There are no native speakers of these languages, but people still study them.

Latin was the language of the Ancient Roman empire, which, at its peak, covered much of southern Europe, north Africa and the Middle East. Eventually, the empire came to an end. The countries that had been part of the Roman empire developed their own languages from Latin. Over time, each language slowly changed, becoming different from the languages in the surrounding countries. The Romance languages are Italian, Spanish, Portuguese, French and Romanian. They are called *Romance* because they developed from Latin, the language of the Romans.

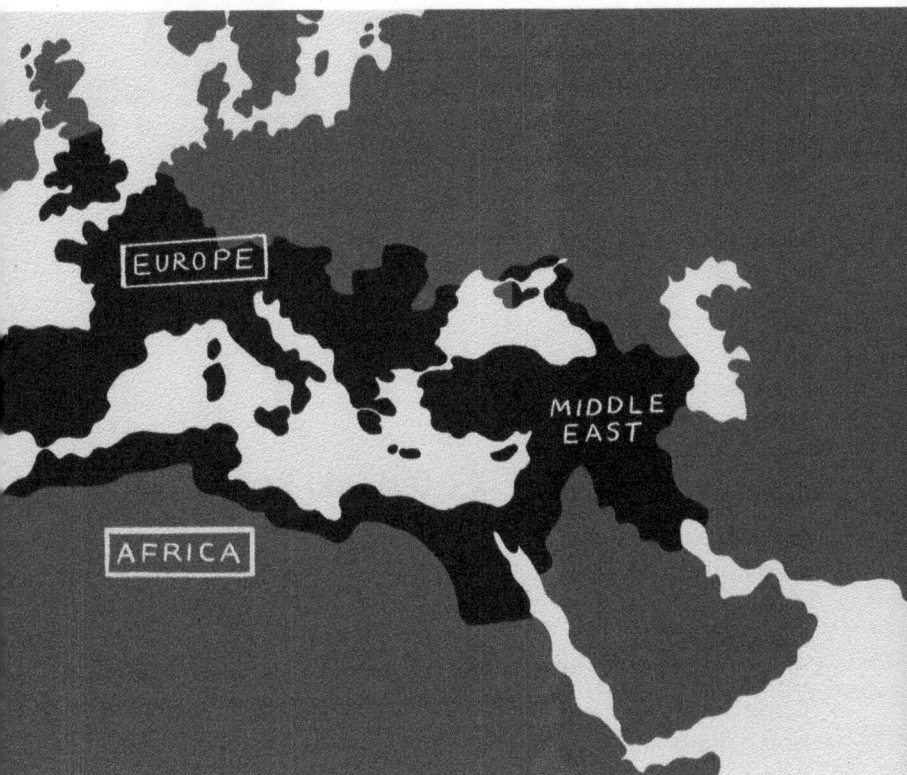

The Roman empire (shown in black)

Even though Latin and Ancient Greek are no longer spoken, they're alive in the words we use today in English, and in other languages.

Did you know?

We use a lot of Latin and Ancient Greek prefixes and suffixes in English. Once you know what they mean, they can help you work out what other words mean.

For example, *tele* is Ancient Greek for 'far', and is the origin for words like *telescope*. *Vis* is Latin for 'sight', which gives us *invisible*, among other words.

You can see where the word *television* came from!

Extinct languages

Unlike dead languages, when a language is *extinct* it means it isn't used at all any more.

Did you know?

There are 573 extinct languages that we know of.

Taíno

Puerto Rico is an island off Central America, with the Caribbean Sea to its south and Atlantic Ocean to its north. Its native language was Taíno, which was also the name given to the people who lived there.

The Taíno language was never written down, but the Taíno people did carve symbols into rocks. These symbols have meanings – a little like the pictograms of Ancient Egypt.

Taíno symbols

Italian navigator Christopher Columbus arrived on the island of Puerto Rico in 1493, on board his ship *Santa María*. It was his second trip across the Atlantic. At this time, the Spanish king and queen wanted to find a faster sea route between Spain and Asia so that they could **import** Asian goods to Europe more quickly.

In the 15th century, all boats heading to Asia from Europe sailed east. Columbus believed if he sailed west from Spain, he could find a faster route. So, with the Spanish monarchs paying for his trip, he set sail – and unexpectedly arrived on Puerto Rico, believing he was in Asia! Instead, he had arrived on land that no one in Europe knew existed: the American continents.

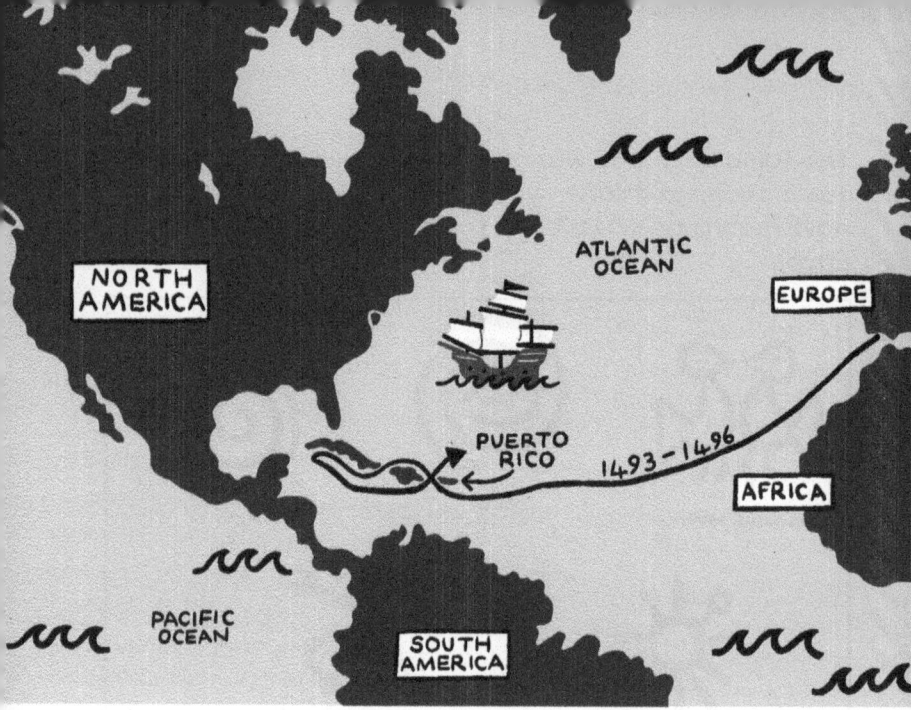

Christopher Columbus's second trip across the Atlantic

Spanish

Columbus's arrival was the start of Spain's colonisation of Puerto Rico, which introduced the Spanish language to the Taíno people. At first, the Taíno language mixed with Spanish, with Taíno words being included in the Spanish that colonisers used on the island. However, within 20 years, the Spanish colonists had forced the Taíno people to speak just Spanish. They **enslaved** the Taíno people and made them work in gold mines.

African languages

Soon after enslaving the native islanders, the colonists brought enslaved people from Africa to work on Puerto Rico. These people spoke different African languages, which introduced African words to the Puerto Rican language, though the official language remained Spanish.

Some African words are still used in Puerto Rican Spanish today.

Language	Word	Meaning
Yoruba (from West Africa)	suku	to comb or style hair
Bantu (from across Africa)	bembé	a celebration, often with music and dance
Wolof (from West Africa)	ñame	a vegetable like a sweet potato
Kimbundu (from Angola)	guaguancó	a music and dance style

English

After 400 years of Spanish rule, the United States of America went to war with Spain and gained control of Puerto Rico. The American government made English the official language, but the islanders kept speaking Spanish, so Spanish and English both became official languages.

Did you know?

The Taíno language never died out completely, as a few Taíno words survived to be used by Puerto Ricans today, and perhaps the most important word is the name of the island itself. Before Spanish colonists named it Puerto Rico, its native Taíno name was *Borikén*, which means 'Land of the Valiant Lord' and is the name still used on the island today.

Did you know?

Today, Puerto Ricans speak a form of Spanish that, because of their history, mixes in English words. They call this language *Spanglish* or *Espanglish*! It's a mix of Spanish and English that makes words that are unique to the island. For example, the Spanish for 'chatting' is *charlando*. In Puerto Rico, this becomes *chateando*:

charlando + *chatting* = *chateando*

My Malagasy nana speaks *Franglais* with my family! *Franglais* is *French* and *English* (the French word for 'English' is *anglais*)!

Puerto Rican language

The unique language spoken on the island is part of Puerto Ricans' identity. It reminds them of how they resisted losing their languages.

Australia

When a language dies, it isn't necessarily lost forever. Dormant languages can be brought back. *Dormant* means 'asleep'!

British and Irish colonists began to arrive in Australia from 1788, bringing the English language with them. They forced the **indigenous** people to speak English, causing native languages to begin to die out.

Barngarla is an indigenous language from southern Australia. The last native speaker of Barngarla died in 1960, but the Barngarla community wanted to wake their sleeping language.

They used a dictionary that had been written in 1844, and added words they remembered their parents and grandparents using to bring their language back. This helped them rediscover their identity and form a link to their ancestors and their **heritage**.

The language today is as close as possible to the Barngarla that was spoken in 1960. However, there was such a gap between the final speaker dying and bringing the language back that it can't be exactly the same – and it has borrowed a lot of words from English. There are no native speakers, but it helps the Barngarla people to feel like a community, with a history that they can now learn about, thanks to understanding the language.

Did you know?

It isn't easy to keep a language alive. Ayapaneco is an indigenous language spoken in Mexico. Following colonisation by Spain, schools began to teach all their classes in Spanish, and local languages started to die out.

Like in Australia, there were people who wanted to create a dictionary, to preserve the Ayapaneco language. However, there were only two native speakers left alive, and they were rumoured to have fallen out, and to have refused to talk to each other for years! They also spoke different versions of the language, so the dictionary includes both versions.

The story has a happy ending though because, not only was a dictionary created, but a classroom was built where the last two Ayapaneco speakers taught children their language.

Malagasy

Do all colonised countries lose their languages? Absolutely not!

Madagascar is the large island off the southeast coast of Africa in the Indian Ocean. The main language of Madagascar is Malagasy. Like all languages, Malagasy has gained words from other languages.

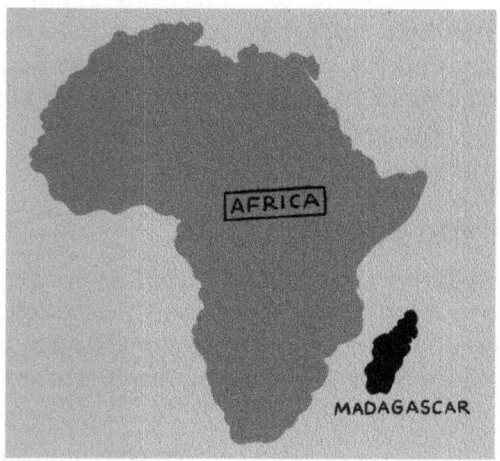

Arabic

Due to its location between Africa and Asia, Arab traders would stop in Madagascar on their journeys importing and exporting goods. They brought their language with them too, of course, and this is where the Malagasy word for 'hello' comes from.

Arabic	Malagasy	English
salam	salama	hello

French

We have seen how some countries colonised others. Madagascar was a colony of France from the 19th century, right up until independence in 1960. Under France's rule, French became the official language, and was the language used in schools.

Upon independence, Malagasy became the official language of Madagascar again, but in the 1980s the Malagasy government decided to switch back to teaching in French. Today, primary schools tend to teach in Malagasy and secondary schools are more likely to use French.

It's not surprising, then, that some French words have been adapted into the Malagasy language.

Here are some Malagasy words that come from French.

French	Malagasy	English
la soupe	lasopy	soup
Allemagne	alemaina	Germany
octobre	oktobra	October
bicyclette	bisikileta	bicycle
savon	savony	soap

Even though Madagascar was colonised and French became its official language for many decades, the native language survived. It absorbed words from French, and from other languages, and Malagasy remains the main language of the inhabitants.

Why keep languages alive?

We try to protect animals from extinction. Languages are part of what makes us human, and it's important to keep them alive too. Every time a language dies, all the stories and knowledge learned in that language die with it.

Take Cherokee, for example, which is the language native to the southern Appalachian Mountains of North America. All the local plants that grow in the area have Cherokee names, and those names tell us whether each plant is edible, poisonous or a medicine. If that language were to die – and it is endangered – then that knowledge could die too.

It's not just knowledge that we could lose – it's our history too. Once a family can no longer read anything written by their grandparents, their link to the people they came from – and therefore their heritage – is broken.

Your own language is part of your identity and culture – what makes you, you!

5 Where is English from?

We've seen that the language spoken in Puerto Rico comes from lots of different languages, and some Malagasy words come from Arabic and French. But where does English come from?

Latin

People in Britain were speaking a language called Brittonic when the Roman invasion in 43 CE expanded the Roman empire to include most of England and Wales and parts of Scotland. The invading Romans brought their language with them: Latin.

People speaking Brittonic started to use Latin words gradually until, over time, they were largely speaking Latin. As the Romans left Britain, their language left with them and Old English took over.

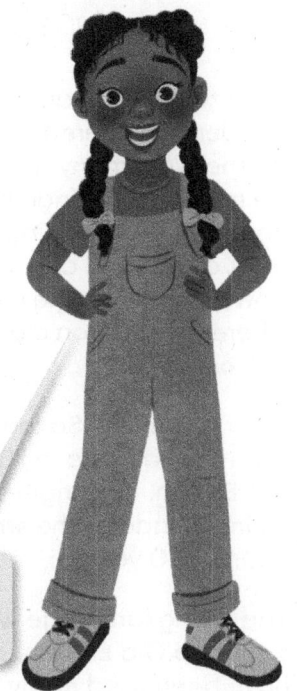

But Latin didn't disappear entirely – it's still in lots of English words we use today.

💡 Did you know?

The Latin for 'hand' is *manus*. These are two very different words, as hand is Old English and *manus* is Latin. Can you think of any words in English that start with *man-* and refer to hands? How about these:

- manufacture = to make something by hand
- manual = work done by hand
- manicure = taking care of your hands

Some of these words have changed a little in meaning over the years – manufacturing is often done by machine now – but can you see how they first came from Latin?

Old English

After the Roman army left in 410 CE, Anglo-Saxon invaders conquered parts of Britain. They came from northern Germany and spoke a Germanic language that we now call Old English. Just as Latin gradually took over from Brittonic, Old English eventually replaced Latin across most of England and its borders with Scotland and Wales. However, the people in Scotland, Wales and Cornwall, where the invasion didn't reach, continued to speak Brittonic.

After the Anglo-Saxon invasion, Viking invaders came from Scandinavia in 793 CE. Unlike the Romans, who had left Britain, the Anglo-Saxons stayed and fought the Viking invaders. The struggle for control of Britain lasted nearly 300 years.

The Viking language was called Old Norse, and was quite similar to Old English, so some Old Norse words would have been used easily by people speaking Old English.

💡 Did you know?

Have you ever noticed how, just like *hand* and *man-*, the names for animals are nothing like their adjectives? For example, something that relates to a cat is *feline* and something that relates to a dog is *canine*; cows are *bovine* and horses are *equine*. We have Old English and Latin to thank for that! The nouns *cat*, *dog*, *cow* and *horse* are Old English words, and their adjectives come from Latin.

Is Old English where today's English comes from? Not quite!

French

There was another invasion, in 1066, when the Norman army of France defeated the English army at the Battle of Hastings. This had quite a big impact on the language spoken in England, because some people began to speak French!

The Bayeux tapestry tells the story of the Battle of Hastings in pictures.

💡 Did you know?

We can see English words that came from French in words such as 'hospital' (*hôpital* in French), 'forest' (*forêt*) and 'arrest' (*arrêt*). These words were originally spelled with an *s*. However, the *s* became silent in French and was eventually dropped, while English kept the *s*.

It's great that speaking English means you know words in other languages! It makes learning languages so much easier.

Today's English

Following the Battle of Hastings, when some people began to use French in England and Wales, others continued to speak English. English has over 170,000 words today, which is more than most languages. One reason for this is that it kept both its Old English and French words, and so has a lot of **synonyms**.

Words that come from Old English tend to sound more informal today, and they are often shorter than French words. For example, *start* comes from Old English. It's shorter and more **colloquial** than *commence*, which means the same thing and comes from French.

As English speakers began to travel and trade more, and met people and saw things they'd never seen before, English gained new words from many other languages.

> ### 💡 Did you know?
> Remember the Taíno language from Puerto Rico? The English words *hammock*, *hurricane* and *canoe* all come from the Taíno language.

British place names

All the invasions that Britain has seen throughout history have left a mark on what we call its towns and villages, as successive invaders named the places where they stayed. And so, today's place names give us a clue to their past.

For example, names ending *-cester*, *-chester* or *-caster*, such as Leicester, Manchester and Lancaster, were Roman forts. Those ending *-burgh* or *-bury*, for example Edinburgh and Canterbury, were also forts, but their names come from Old English.

We can even go back earlier than the Roman invasion. Many places in Scotland and Wales include *inver* or *aber*, which mean 'mouth of the river' and come from Brittonic. They give us place names including Inverness ('mouth of the River Ness'), Aberdeen ('mouth of the River Don') and Abertawe ('mouth of the River Tawe'), which is Welsh for Swansea.

Early Anglo-Saxon villages were often named after the leader of the tribe who lived there. The beginning of the place name was the name of the leader, followed by *-ing* or *-folk*, which mean 'people'. For example, the village of a leader called Redda would be *Redda + ing = Redding*, which became *Reading*.

This also works for -*ham*, meaning 'home' in Old English, so *Fulla's home* became *Fulham*, and -*ton*, referring to 'farm', gave us *Kingston* ('King's farm').

Sometimes, more than one ending can be used for a single place name, so *Orpington* comes from *Orped's people's farm*.

Some place names are a little more obvious. The *Sand-* from *Sandwich* does refer to a beach; -*wich* is an Old English trading place, and so *Sandwich* was originally a market near the coast.

> **Did you know?**
>
> If the place was named Sandwich because it was a coastal market town, how did it also become the name of something we eat? The food was named after the 4th Earl of Sandwich, who may have invented the sandwich. However, the 1st Earl chose his title because Sandwich was a major port when he was made an earl. If he had lived more recently, perhaps today's most popular lunch would be a ham-and-cheese Felixstowe (Felixstowe is the biggest and busiest port in Britain)!

All this history means that today's English has its roots in Old English with some words from French, Latin and other languages mixed in! And of course, English is now spoken in many countries around the world, where it continues to evolve and change.

Let's have a look at some of those countries.

6 Anglophone countries

Anglophone refers to a country where English is a main language.

> ### 💡 Did you know?
> Where does the word *anglophone* come from?
>
> *Anglia* is the Latin name for England. *Phone* was originally an Ancient Greek word. It translates as 'speaker' or 'voice', and it's where we get words like *telephone*, *microphone* and *phoneme*.
>
> So *anglophone* means 'speaking English'!

There are more than 80 countries around the world where English is an official language, and there are some English-speaking countries on every continent (except for Antarctica).

Accents

People in anglophone countries may speak the same language, but does English sound the same everywhere it's spoken?

Britain

For a small country, Britain has a staggering range of different accents. Accents vary in Britain as you move from north to south and from west to east. How did this happen?

The Anglo-Saxon invasion of England involved three main tribes:

- The Angles who settled mostly in northern England and the Midlands;
- The Jutes who settled in the southeast;
- The Saxons who settled in the south.

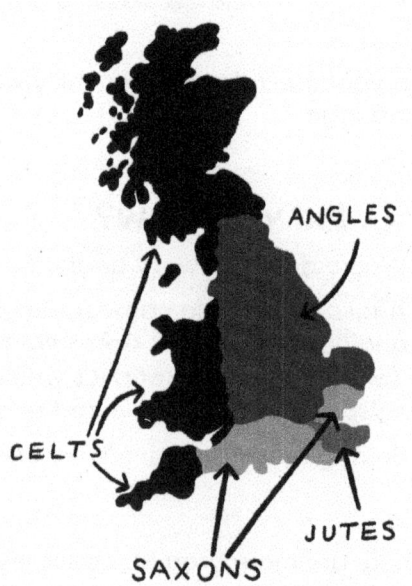

Tribes in Britain after the Anglo-Saxon invasions

Over time, the different versions of Old English that the tribes spoke gradually developed into the different English accents that we hear today. Scottish, Welsh and Cornish accents developed out of their different Celtic languages including Gaelic, as the Anglo-Saxons largely didn't settle in Scotland, Wales or Cornwall.

America and Australia

Britain began to colonise America in 1607. Therefore, the first people to speak English in the United States had British accents. So why are American accents so different from British ones today?

English doesn't just *sound* different across the world – it *is* different!

Once English speakers began to settle in the United States, they no longer heard how English was being spoken in Britain, and so the two forms of the language developed separately.

At the same time, British families mingled with Native Americans, African Americans and colonists from other parts of Europe, and American accents grew out of all these different ways of speaking.

Meanwhile, something similar was happening in Australia. British and Irish colonists began to arrive from 1788. Like in America, their accents blended with each other's – and with indigenous and German accents – to form a new way of speaking that developed separately from that used in the British Isles.

British and American vocabulary

Have you noticed that American English and British English are not the same? Some words are spelled differently, such as 'color' instead of 'colour'. And some words are completely different in these two versions of English.

Streets

What do you call the side of the road where people walk? If you use British English, you'll call it the *pavement*, but if your English is American, then you'll say *sidewalk*. Why is this?

Back in the 17th century, when American English was forming, there weren't many pavements. In those days, carts, horses and people normally all used the same road space. So, in the early days, American English didn't need a word for pavement. Later on, when pavements became common, American English developed its own word – *sidewalk*, from the *side* of the road where people *walk*.

Pavement comes from the Latin *pavimentum*, which means 'trodden down floor'.

Clothing

There can be some confusion when British and American people talk about what they wear! Someone using American English will call *pants* what in Britain are *trousers*. In both countries, they were originally *pantaloons*, which was shortened to *pants* in America, while Britain adopted *trousers* from **Gaelic**.

Water

We know that lots of English words come from French. Where do you get water from in a kitchen or bathroom? If you speak American English, you'll call it a *faucet*, while in British English, it's a *tap*.

Faucet comes from a medieval French word (*fausset*) while *tap* comes from Old English (*taeppa*) – and both mean the same thing (a tap on a barrel)! But what's the water called that comes out? It's *tap water* in both Britain and America!

New Zealand vocabulary

New Zealand is a country off the southeast coast of Australia in the Pacific Ocean. Although most people speak English, its indigenous language is Māori (also called *te reo Māori*), and both languages are spoken there.

The Māori language arrived in New Zealand around the 13th century, when explorers from Polynesia discovered the islands and decided to settle there.

English was first spoken there when James Cook, a British navigator, reached New Zealand in 1769. It became a British colony in 1840, and independent in 1947.

> My grandpa is Māori, so I can speak some of the language! Let's have a look at a few words.

Māori and English are two very different languages. However, if you listen to New Zealanders speaking English, you will hear them use a lot of Māori words.

- kia ora / kia ora e hoa = hello / goodbye / thank you (also wishes the person you're talking to good health)

- Māori = Māori (referring to indigenous inhabitants, their **descendants** and the language)

- Pākehā = anyone with European heritage

- Aotearoa = land of the long white cloud (New Zealand)

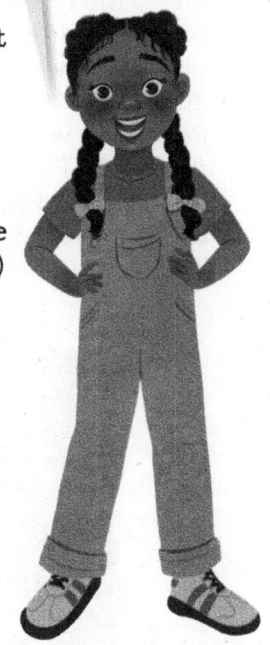

New Zealand English is an example of the way a language grows and develops by gaining new words from another language; in this case, Māori. These new words allow people to communicate about things that are particular to New Zealand, especially relating to Māori culture. A lot of the words don't have a direct equivalent in English and are best communicated in Māori.

☼ Did you know?

New Zealand was named by Europeans after the Dutch province of Zeeland, but its original Māori name is *Aotearoa*.

☼ Did you know?

Kiwi is the name of the national bird of New Zealand. It is also a nickname for all New Zealanders, whether Māori or Pākehā! It was originally used during the First World War for New Zealand soldiers, and since then to refer to anyone of New Zealand nationality.

A kiwi

Let's return to the British Isles and learn more about the languages spoken there today.

7 Indigenous British languages

As we've seen, English isn't the only language in English-speaking countries. Although most people in the British Isles speak English, there are several other native languages spoken there too.

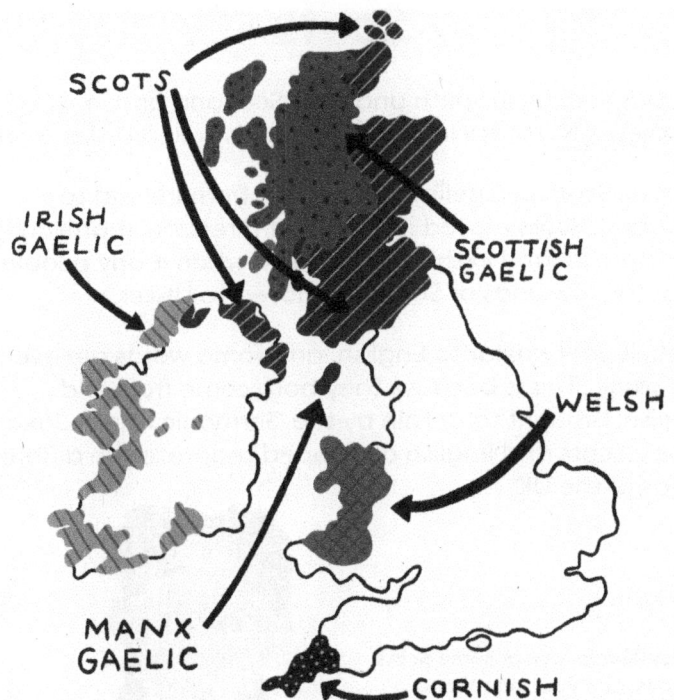

Indigenous languages in the British Isles

Scottish Gaelic

Gaelic arrived in Argyllshire in Scotland when settlers who spoke Gaelic moved from Ireland in around 500 CE.

Scottish Gaelic is mainly spoken in the Highlands and the Islands off the west coast of Scotland. Like many languages, it didn't stay just in Scotland. It is also spoken in Canada, due to migration from Scotland in the 18th and 19th centuries.

Scots

Scots is spoken in south and east Scotland and in northeast Northern Ireland, where it is called Ulster-Scots.

Just as Scottish Gaelic was brought from Ireland to Scotland, Scots moved in the other direction. It arrived in Northern Ireland in the 17th century, when many people from the lowlands of Scotland moved to Ulster.

Scots is very similar to English, and some words are even the same. This is because they both come from Old English, brought to Britain by the Germanic Anglo-Saxon tribes. Scots and English developed separately in different areas of the UK.

Let's have a look at some Scots words. Can you understand what they mean?

🔆 Did you know?

Here are some Scots words. How many do you recognise?

- aye = yes / always
- bairn / wean = child
- blether = idle chat
- crack = news
- smirr = a fine rain
- teemin = pouring
- wee = little
- eejit = idiot (when Roald Dahl's book *The Twits* was translated into Scots, its title became *The Eejits*)

Irish Gaelic

Irish Gaelic is spoken mainly in the west of Ireland, but all road signs in the whole of the Republic of Ireland are in both Irish Gaelic and English.

Did you know? 🔆

Remember the Spanglish (mix of Spanish and English) spoken in Puerto Rico? In Ireland, there's a language known as Hiberno-English, which mixes Irish Gaelic and English in much the same way.

Manx Gaelic

Manx Gaelic is spoken on the Isle of Man, which is an island that sits in the Irish Sea, between Ireland, Scotland, England and Wales. This language originally came from the Irish Gaelic spoken by the people who also took Gaelic to Scotland. Today's Manx is very similar to Irish and Scottish Gaelic.

Most people who lived on the Isle of Man spoke Manx right up to the 19th century, when English started to take over. To ensure it isn't lost, Manx is taught today in schools on the island.

Did you know?

The Manx name for the Isle of Man is Mannin, which means 'Manannán's Island'. Manannán is a sea god from Irish and Manx mythology who, the myth says, was the island's first ruler.

Welsh

Welsh, which is spoken across most of Wales, is a direct descendant of Brittonic, the language that was spoken in Britain when the Roman invasion occurred. People across England and the border with Wales started to speak Latin, but the Welsh language survived the invasion.

Road sign in Wales

English is also spoken throughout Wales, and both are the official languages of the country. Today, almost a quarter of Welsh school children go to schools that teach their lessons in Welsh.

Cornish

Cornish is the native language of Cornwall in southwest England. Like Welsh, it is a direct descendant of Brittonic. Despite its long history stretching thousands of years, it has only officially been recognised by the UK* government since 2002! Fewer than 1,000 people speak it fluently, and the last person whose only language was Cornish died in 1777. However, some Cornish people who know a few words like to use them every day.

💡 Did you know?

An interesting fact about Cornish is that there are more Cornish speakers in London than in Cornwall! A lot of Cornish people move to London for work, and they find Cornish lessons available there, which help them connect to their heritage.

They may say 'hello' (*dydh da* – say: *dyth-**dah***) and 'goodbye' (*duw genes* – say: *dew-**ghen**-ez*) in Cornish, but hold the rest of the conversation in English.

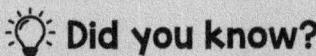

Road sign in Cornwall

*UK = United Kingdom of England, Scotland, Wales and Northern Ireland

Let's have a look at another language we speak in my family: Nepali.

8 Culture

The languages we speak form part of our identity.

When we learn words in another language, we start learning something about the culture and identity of the people who speak that language.

Nepali

Nepali is the language of Nepal. Nepal is situated between China and India, and is the location of the world's highest mountain, Mount Everest.

In English, we have the word 'you'. We use it no matter who we're speaking to, or how many people there are.

When talking in the Nepali language, the speaker chooses their words to indicate how much respect they are showing. Respect is extremely important in Nepali culture.

Ta means 'you' and shows low respect. It is used with close friends and people younger than the speaker. *Timi* also means 'you'. It shows medium respect and is used with people the speaker doesn't know well and who are a similar age. To show high respect, *tapai* is used with people older than the speaker, such as parents and teachers.

Untranslatable words

We have looked at words in other languages and what they mean in English. This is called *translation*. However, as we saw in Māori, some languages have words that can't easily be translated into another language. These words can teach us something about the people who speak them.

Cherokee

Cherokee is an indigenous language, native to the southern Appalachian Mountains of North America.

The Cherokee word *oo-kah-huh-sdee* describes the feeling of delight when you see a cute baby or kitten. Although we have no single word for this emotion in English, the Tagalog language, which is spoken in the Philippines, does have a word: *gigil*.

On the other hand, there are words in English that have no direct Cherokee translation. For example, Cherokee has no word that means 'goodbye'; it only has the word *donadagohvi*, which means 'I will see you again'.

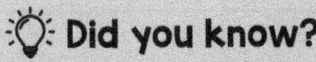

Did you know?
Donadagohvi is similar to the French for 'goodbye', *au revoir*, which translates as 'until we see each other again'.

Danish

Danish is spoken in Denmark, a Scandinavian country in northern Europe.

Isn't that a lovely way to say goodbye?

There is one word above all others that sums up Danish culture, and that word is *hygge*. Like the Cherokee and Tagalog words on page 49, there is no single English word that translates *hygge*, which describes the warm feeling of being cosy at home with friends or family, perhaps under a blanket by a fire, or any other situation that causes the same emotions.

Lost in translation

Let's have a look at a few more untranslatable words.

Language	Word	Meaning
Georgian	shemomedjamo	When you eat something even though you're not hungry – because it's so delicious
Indonesian	jayus	A joke so terrible that you have to laugh; like a dad joke
Indonesian	mencolek	When you trick someone by tapping their opposite shoulder from where you're standing
Japanese	age-otori	A disaster haircut that makes you look worse than before
Inuit	iktsuarpok	Repeatedly going outside to check if someone is coming because you're excited to see them

Oral traditions

If you have any family stories that your relatives like to tell and retell, you may notice that sometimes one part is emphasised and other bits left out. The stories may change a little each time they're told. They probably aren't written down, but may be a regular part of family celebrations. This is an oral tradition.

> Our family stories change depending on who's telling them, because the speaker always makes their own part in the story bigger!

Have you ever played a game where you whisper a message from player to player then compare the final message with the original? Oral communication can be misheard or misunderstood and get changed. Oral traditions can work in the same way, with stories gradually changing over time.

North America

Many Native American tribes did not use writing until hundreds or thousands of years after it was first invented. Oral storytelling is important for remembering and passing on history, science and traditions, and for older people to teach younger ones. Parents enjoy telling their children traditional stories as a way of continuing their communities' cultures. Stories can also serve as warnings about dangerous behaviour.

For example, parents can warn their young children from wandering onto dangerous sea ice by telling a traditional Native American tale about a sea monster who grabs children within reach and puts them in its pouch. This is a way of keeping young children safe, away from freezing water.

The Qalupalik, an Inuit sea monster

Australia

Oral traditions are important among the indigenous people in Australia too. The Wardaman people of Australia's Northern Territory connect to their ancestors and tell the stories of their origins through speech and song.

Africa and the Caribbean

Some cultures, such as the Akan people from West Africa, use oral tradition to teach history, duty and skills, as well as to pass on myths and legends. Remembering, telling and updating stories is also a way of improving memory and sharpening the imagination.

> My favourite Anansi story is 'Anansi and the World's Stories'. See if you can find it or read another Anansi story.

One well-known African-Caribbean series of stories, traditionally passed down orally, is that of Anansi the spider. These tales of wisdom, knowledge and trickery began in Ghana and have been kept alive in the community as people, often enslaved, were taken across the Atlantic Ocean to America and the Caribbean.

Hearing stories of a character who uses cunning, creativity and wit to outsmart more powerful opponents gave people hope, as well as a link to their past and heritage.

Today, the stories allow communities to connect with their ancestors. Parents often update the topics to a modern setting and use them to warn their children of dangers, just like the sea monster in North America. Today, however, the warnings may be of online dangers, or the perils of not doing your homework!

Language changes

We have seen how writing led to many new inventions as knowledge spread. But it's not just objects that are invented – words are too, as language itself is constantly changing. New words are called *neologisms*.

Each time a new device or way of using technology is invented, a word is needed to describe it. *Television*, *internet* and *meme* were all new words once!

Sometimes people invent words when they have new ideas and can't quite find an existing word to mean what they want to say. Often, two words are pushed together to form a new word. This is called a *portmanteau*.

Which words do you use that your parents don't use or understand? These words are probably neologisms!

Some examples of portmanteaus from recent years are:

- floordrobe
- hangry
- adorkable.

Have you heard any of these words? Do you know what they mean? Do you still hear people using them, or are they old-fashioned now?

William Shakespeare

Shakespeare was a British playwright and poet who lived in England in the 16th century. You may know his plays *Romeo and Juliet*, *A Midsummer Night's Dream* or *The Tempest*.

Shakespeare's writing shows how much language changes, because

William Shakespeare

although we can recognise it as English, it is very different from how we speak and write today. However, did you know that Shakespeare invented over 1,700 new words and phrases that he put in his plays? We use many of them today, including:

- bedroom = room for sleeping, which has a bed
- downstairs = lower floor, down some steps
- fair play = follow rules / treat people equally
- gossip = talk about other people
- rant = speak angrily for a long time.

Roald Dahl

Roald Dahl was a British children's writer who lived in the 20th century. His most famous books include *Charlie and the Chocolate Factory*, *Matilda* and *The Twits*. Like Shakespeare, he also invented neologisms: around 500 names and other new words.

How do people understand new words the first time they're used? Perhaps you have seen a made-up word in a story you're reading. You probably understand it by **context** and by knowing similar words.

Some of Dahl's neologisms are *onomatopoeic* – they sound like their meaning. This helps us understand words like *phizz-whizzing*, which means 'excellent' or 'splendid', because it sounds energetic and exciting. Others sound a bit like words we already know. *Scrumdiddlyumptious* describes utterly delicious food, and it has the same suffix as 'delicious', which helps us understand it's like delicious, but exaggerated. Some of Dahl's words are really fun to say and make us want to keep reading, like *biffsquiggled* (confused or puzzled).

Can you make up your own word that other people could understand just by hearing it or seeing it written down? Can you put it in a sentence?

I like making up my own words too! I take words from the different languages my family speak and mix them up to make new ones, like *pleuving*, which is French for 'rain' but with an English ending!

9 Printing

From speaking to writing

Earlier, we looked at how people first began to write, but what did they write on? The first writing was on clay tablets in Mesopotamia, while in Ancient Egypt it was painted on pottery and carved in stone. This is text that you couldn't easily carry around with you, unlike the portable electronic devices, notepads and books we keep in our pockets and bags today. In addition, writing was quite rare as few people knew how to write. Early writing wasn't much use for shopping lists, but wealthy people like kings and pharaohs could use it to keep permanent records.

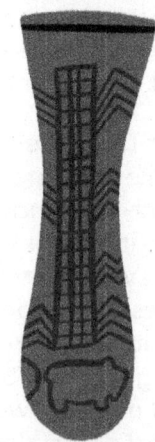

Ancient Egyptian vase painted with symbols of animals, the River Nile and the mounds located either side of the river

The invention of paper

Once the Egyptian people realised how useful writing was, they needed something to write on that was cheaper and easier to carry around than clay tablets and stone.

Papyrus

Papyrus is a plant that grows all along the banks of the River Nile in Egypt, so there is a lot of it! Ancient Egyptian people realised that they could make a material from it that they could write on. This was the first paper!

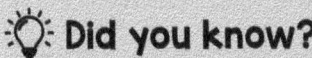 Did you know?

How did the Egyptians make paper from papyrus?

1. Take the stalk of the papyrus plant and peel the green skin from it.
2. Slice the inside of the stalk into long strips.
3. Flatten the strips using a rolling pin.
4. Soak them in water for two weeks.
5. Arrange them in a lattice pattern by placing slices alternately from left to right and top to bottom.
6. Cover the lattice with a piece of fabric.
7. Place it under a heavy press for a week.

It was a long process but, at the end of it, the Egyptians had the world's first paper!

Papyrus scroll

The Ancient Egyptians made so much paper that they were able to export it to other countries. Then, in 30 BCE, the Roman empire conquered Egypt.

The Roman conquerors saw how useful paper was and began to sell it all over the Roman empire – which covered an enormous area by this time. Paper became so much cheaper and more widely available in the Roman empire that bookshops and libraries started to open. The books at this time still didn't look like ours – they were scrolls made of papyrus – but they were written texts that people could carry around with them, and so we can call them books.

Parchment

When the Roman empire collapsed in the 5th century, papyrus was no longer available to Europeans. A new type of paper called *parchment*, made from animal skin, was invented, but it cost a lot and was much slower to write on than papyrus. This made books very expensive – the same as the price of a house – and so they were very rare in Europe at that time.

When books began to disappear, education became more difficult and there were fewer new discoveries. In Europe, this period became known as the Dark Ages. Meanwhile, in Asia, science and culture were flourishing in the Islamic Golden Age.

Did you know?

The spine of the animal used to make parchment was visible on the writing surface and was the place where the parchment was folded – this is why the edge of a book where the pages join is called its *spine*.

Parchment is extremely hard-wearing, and some books made from it can last hundreds of years.

Paper in China

While the people of the Egyptian and Roman empires were writing on papyrus, Chinese people had invented paper made from mulberry trees in the 2nd century CE. Although parchment had become scarce and expensive in Europe, paper was cheap and plentiful in China. For 600 years, only people in China knew how to make paper. That continued until the year 751, when Arab armies from the Middle East defeated China in battle and discovered paper among the possessions of the defeated Chinese troops. This discovery led to writing materials becoming widely available once again, which, in turn, allowed knowledge to spread.

In the 9th century, a method of printing on paper was invented in China. It used wooden blocks with text carved out that allowed multiple copies of a text to be made. This invention caused an explosion in the spread of knowledge as books on different topics, such as medicine and farming, were produced. Outside China, no one knew about printing at that time.

The invention of the printing press

Before printing was invented, making books was a time-consuming process as all books had to be written by hand. Not only did making copies take a really long time, but it was very expensive and the **scribes** who copied the text could easily make mistakes. All of this meant that books were rare in Europe between about the 5th and 15th centuries.

Johannes Gutenberg was a German inventor and craftsman who wanted to speed up the time it took to make books. In 1448, he invented the printing press – a machine that printed words on to paper.

> **Did you know?**
> Printing presses used a system where typesetters would place all the letters that made up the words they were printing onto a metal plate, ready for the ink. All the letters were kept in separate drawers called *cases*, with capital letters stored above small letters. That's why, today, we call capital letters *upper case* and small letters *lower case*.

Literacy

Once the printing press was invented, texts could be produced quicker and on a larger scale. It meant that information on a huge range of topics could be spread to a wide range of people. And now that there was so much text available, many more people were able to learn to read. Reading became central to education as students could study books on all subjects. Reading also became a form of entertainment, as people started to read for enjoyment.

Printing was the start of people reading the news too – not just from their local area, but from across the world. This hadn't been possible before the printing press because writing individual copies by hand took so long. Suddenly, multiple copies could be made at once.

Spelling

The printing press influenced language itself. Before printed books, no one could agree on the best way to spell words. Even people's names had no single spelling. When people who couldn't read or write had to give their name to an official, the official would write down what they heard in the way they thought best.

My last name is Feldwick. We've seen old records where it's spelled Fieldwick and even Veldvick!

Even those who could write varied how they wrote their names: William Shakespeare spelled his name in different ways, including Shakspere and Shakspeare. Once writing was in print, the same spellings could be taught to everyone and spelling rules became more permanent. This was helped by the first dictionary, which was published in 1755. However, like language itself, spelling gradually changes over time.

The Scientific Revolution

One area that benefitted from the spread of knowledge was science. For thousands of years, people making scientific discoveries found it difficult to share their findings, or to learn what other scientists had discovered. In the 16th and 17th centuries, printing allowed the results of experiments to be published and shared in a reliable way, without errors introduced by scribes. Now, scientists could build on the discoveries that had been made before them, and science suddenly made huge progress. This was called the Scientific Revolution.

The Industrial Revolution

The printing press was the first example of a machine doing work previously done by people. This, combined with the spread of knowledge that printing allowed, led to the Industrial Revolution (1760-1840). Factories were built, and products that had been made by hand could now be produced by machines in huge quantities. Just as the printing press produced lots of books, making other products was suddenly much quicker and cheaper. Looking back, we now believe that the printing press started the modern age of science and industry (although no one was aware of this at the time).

Ultimately, the printing press led to the invention of the typewriter, which allowed writers to type directly on to paper. Eventually, computers were invented, followed by all the devices we use today.

Modern devices, such as phones and tablets, allow us to type and read text and books on screens. The printing press was the beginning of typing but it has eventually led us to digital text and reduced the need to print.

All this technology from the invention of printing!

10 Other kinds of languages

Sign language

Now you know all about spoken and written languages, but what other types of languages are there?

Do you know anyone who is deaf or hard of hearing? How do they communicate? Many deaf people use sign language. Sign language is a way of communicating using hand gestures, facial expressions and **body language**, and it is how many deaf people express themselves. It has different words and grammar from spoken languages, so it is not the same as the language that is spoken in the area where the sign language is used. Just as people who speak the same language are part of a community, people who use the same sign language form a community too.

Everything that people say using words can be communicated using sign language. In fact, as we have already discovered, humans' first communication was using gestures and signs, before they were even able to speak. So, sign language is older than spoken language!

Sign languages have a lot in common with spoken languages. In deaf families, babies learn to sign by copying the people around them, just as babies in hearing families learn to speak by repeating the sounds they hear. When people speak, they sometimes use a different tone of voice to show meaning, for example they might talk loudly to show anger. In the same way, sign languages aren't made up of just hand gestures; facial expressions communicate meaning as well. And while spoken languages change as new words are invented, sign languages change too.

Sign languages around the world

Just like spoken languages, sign languages vary around the world, and people from different countries may not understand each other unless they have learned each other's language. The most used sign language in the world is American Sign Language, which is common in America, Canada, Mexico, Africa and Asia.

British Sign Language (BSL) is the most used sign language in the UK. It was only officially recognised as its own language in 2003, but people had already been using it for over 300 years by then! Just as English is an official language in Australia and New Zealand – with differences from the way it is spoken in the UK – Auslan (Australian Sign Language) and NZSL (New Zealand Sign Language) are similar to BSL.

BSL has become better known among hearing people since 2021 when Rose Ayling-Ellis, an actor who is deaf, appeared on the British television programme *Strictly Come Dancing*, using a sign-language interpreter to communicate, as well as signing and speaking herself. This led to a surge in people searching for 'sign language' online and signing up for classes.

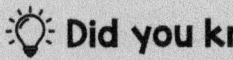 Did you know?

There are over 300 different sign languages around the world.

150,000 people use BSL in the UK.

Signs in BSL

Hello

Sorry

Thank you

Clapping / applauding

Hand signals in sport

Who else uses gestures to communicate? Do you ever watch sports like football and cricket? The referee or umpire needs to communicate with a lot of people at once. The players on both teams, their managers and coaches, and the crowd watching the match all need to understand the official's decisions, but in such a large, noisy place, speaking or shouting just won't work. So, a bit like sign language, referees use their hands.

Unlike sign language, though, these gestures need to be big and clear, so that they can be seen from far away.

Football (soccer)

Goal

Corner kick

Pushing

Elbowing

Football referees' signals can be easily understood by most people as lots of them look like a mime of what the referee is saying. Look at the signals for pushing and elbowing, for example.

Cricket

Cricket umpires, on the other hand, use less obvious signals. Although some look like a mime, no one really knows where others came from as they have been used for hundreds of years. Like any game, everyone who plays cricket agrees on the rules and learns what the umpires' signals mean.

Out

Wide

Four runs

Six runs

Computer languages

Most languages are both spoken and written down. Some, like sign language, are visual and are not written down. But are there any languages that are written but never spoken? Computer programmers create new games and software by typing a special code that a computer can understand. You may have used Scratch to create games or websites. This is a type of computer language.

When computer programs were first invented, they used numbers and complicated sums to make a computer work. Grace Hopper was an early computer scientist who programmed computers for the United States Navy during the Second World War. She was the first person to invent a computer program that used English words, making programming much easier.

If you were learning a new language, would you rather learn one that used words or numbers?

What happens when you are talking to someone and you use the wrong word, or get a bit mixed up and your words come out in the wrong order? The person you are talking to may not know what you mean. Or, how about when you're typing a message and autocorrect changes a word to something that you don't mean? The person reading the message may not understand it. It's the same with computer programs – one tiny mistake and the computer will not be able to run your program. This is called a *bug*.

 Did you know?

Grace Hopper invented the term *debugging* (meaning to fix a computer program) when a moth that flew into a computer had to be removed for the computer to work. This is an example of a neologism that is now used all the time.

Artificial intelligence

Computers use language to understand what programmers want them to do. But there are other ways that computers interact with language.

Using artificial intelligence (AI), computers and apps can help people who speak different languages to understand each other. There are translation tools that allow users to type in text and the app will translate it into another language. Or you can speak into a device, and it will play audio of what you have said in another language.

AI uses enormous networks of millions of examples of sentences to learn how to translate between different languages.

By analysing millions of sentences, AI can improve the results of its translation to sound more natural in the language it's translating into. This is just like how people learn a new language – by reading and listening to others who have been speaking and writing the language their whole life.

Language and literacy

So, is it important that we learn about language? Yes! We have seen that languages and communication – reading, writing, speaking and listening – are a part of our identity and what make us human. Robots can help us communicate with each other, but even the best ones can't replace human language.

Now that you've learned all about language and literacy, are you going to start learning a new language? Would you like to learn a language that is dying? How about a different type of language, like a computer language or sign language? Perhaps you'd like to be a writer of songs, stories or poems, or a non-fiction writer. Maybe one day you will write a book, like the one you've just been reading!

> I'd like to be a translator, helping people who speak different languages.

Glossary

accents	the way words are pronounced in a particular country or area
ancestors	people who came before us who we are related to
body language	communicating without words using body movements
colloquial	language that isn't formal
colonised	settled in another place and took control of it
context	words around a word that help the reader to understand its meaning
descendants	people or languages that come directly from other people or languages
enslaved	forced someone to work for and obey someone else without being paid
evolved	gradually changed
export	sell things overseas
fossils	remains of an ancient person, animal or plant
heritage	the history and culture of a group of people that has been passed down through the years
hieroglyph	symbol that represents an object or sound
hieroglyphics	writing made up of hieroglyphs
import	bring things from overseas to sell
indigenous	originally from a particular place; similar to *native*

native	originally from a particular place; similar to *indigenous*
pharaoh	king or queen of Ancient Egypt
scribes	people whose job was to copy documents by hand
synonyms	words that mean the same as other words, e.g. *near* and *close*
taxes	money that residents of a place have to pay the government so it can provide public services
traders	people who buy and sell things
verbally	using spoken words

Index

alphabet 14-18
Ancient Egypt 12-13, 14-15, 56-57
Ancient Romans 16, 21, 31, 32, 35, 38, 57-58
Brittonic 31, 32, 35, 46, 47
Cherokee 30, 49
clay tablets 11, 56
colonisation 19-20, 24, 26, 27, 29, 39, 41
computing 67-68
cuneiform 11
dead languages 20-22
dormant languages 26-27
extinct languages 22-26
heritage 25, 30, 47, 53
hieroglyphics 12-13

human evolution 3-4
language family trees 7-9
Māori 6, 41-42
Mesopotamia 10-11, 12, 13, 56
neologisms 53-55
paper 56-59
papyrus 57-58
parchment 58
pictograms 12, 14, 15
printing 59-60
sign language 63-67
storytelling 51-53
Taíno 22-26, 35
translation 49-50, 68-69
word order 6

Now answer the questions ...

1. In what three ways do apes communicate?
2. 'Over time, humans have gradually invented and improved these items'. Think of another word or phrase that could be used instead of 'gradually' in this sentence on page 4.
3. If the Normans had not invaded England, what do you think would have been the effect on the English language?
4. What does the word 'forced' on page 26 tell us about how British colonists treated indigenous people?
5. Why do you think the author included a map on page 43?
6. What is one reason we have lots of synonyms in English?
7. Sum up why we need hand signals in sport.
8. What do you think has had the biggest impact on the English language?